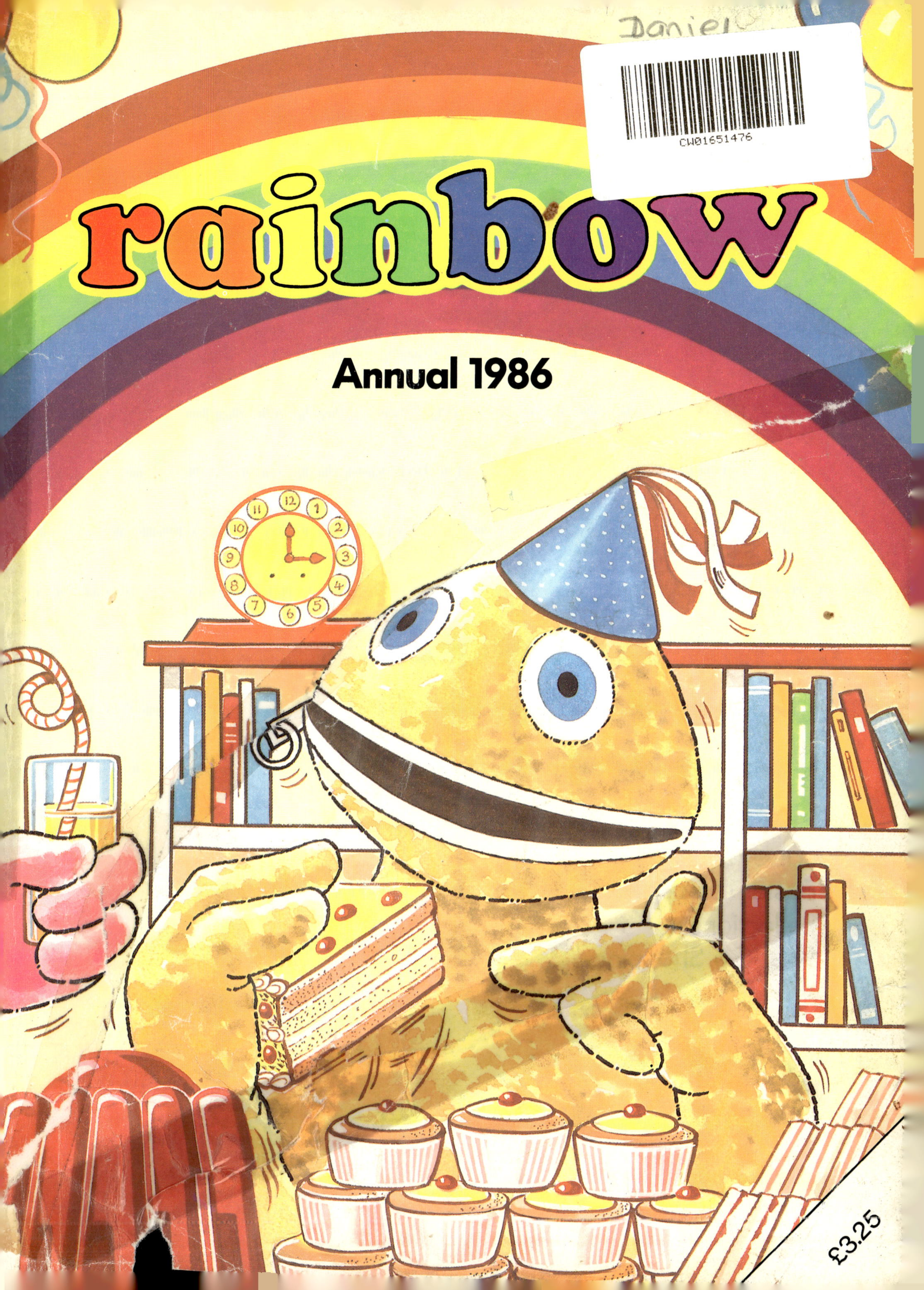
Daniel
CW01651476
rainbow
Annual 1986
£3.25

CONTENTS

Published in Great Britain by Wo International Publishing Limited., P.O. Box 111, Great Ducie Street, Manchester M60 3BL.
Printed in Italy.
BN 7235 6749 2.

The Lost Puppy

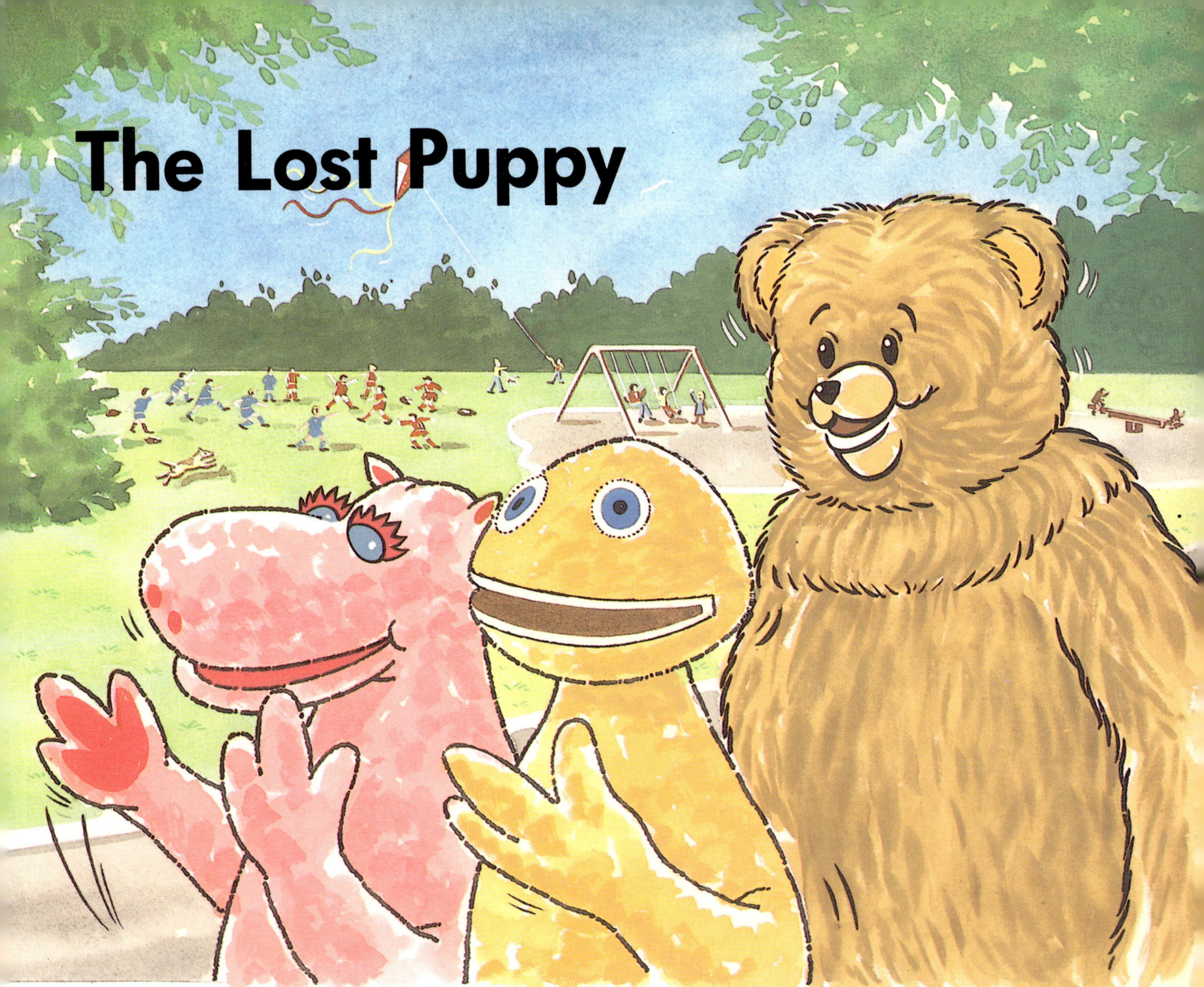

It is a lovely hot sunny day, and Bungle, Zippy and George have decided to go for a walk in the park. There are a lot of people there. Some are playing football, some are swinging on the swings, and some are just sitting on the grass enjoying the sunshine.

"Isn't this nice?" says George as they walk along. "I do like going for walks in the park."

"Yes, so do I," says Bungle. "And the sunshine is lovely too."

"Look," says Zippy. "There's an icecream van over there. Shall we have an icecream?"

Bungle and George laugh. "You're always hungry, Zippy!" says Bungle. "But an icecream would be very nice on a hot day like today."

They go over to the icecream van.

"Hello Bungle, Zippy and George," says the man who sells the icecreams. "What would you like?"

"Three cornets," says Bungle. "And can we have some chocolate sauce over the top, please?"

"Of course you can," says the man, and he gives the three friends a cornet filled with lovely cold icecream, and chocolate sauce on the top.

"Yummy, yummy," says Zippy, licking his icecream. "I do love icecream!"

Just behind them is a little girl, with a puppy on a lead.

"Oh, what a lovely puppy!" says George. "What's his name?"

"His name is Max," says the little girl. "Mummy and Daddy gave him to me for my birthday, and I *do* love him."

The puppy gives a friendly bark, and looks up at Zippy's icecream.

"You can't have any of this," says Zippy. "This is my icecream."

"He loves icecream," says the little girl. "It's his favourite food."

She buys an ice lolly and goes off with the puppy.

"We must go home soon," says Bungle. "Geoffrey will be waiting for us. We can eat our icecreams as we go."

So they set off for home, eating their icecreams. The sun is very hot, and it begins to melt their icecreams as they walk along.

"Look, Zippy," says George. "Your icecream is melting and dripping on to the pavement."

"Oh no!" says Zippy. "I'll have to eat it very fast so that I don't waste any more!"

He gobbles it up very fast indeed. Greedy Zippy!

When they get home, Geoffrey is waiting for them. "Hello," he says. "Isn't it a lovely day?"

"Oh yes!" says George. "We went to the park this

afternoon, and had icecreams there!"

"And we met a little girl with a puppy called Max," says Bungle. "Max likes icecream almost as much as Zippy does."

"He tried to eat mine," says Zippy.

"No, he didn't," says Bungle, laughing. "But he would have liked to."

Just then, they hear a scratching, snuffling sound at the door.

"What's that?" says George. "Is it a ghost?"

"No, of course not," says Geoffrey. "There's no such thing. It's someone at the door."

He goes to the door and opens it. Outside on the step sits a very small puppy, with its lead trailing behind it.

"It's Max!" says Bungle. "But where's the little girl he belongs to?"

"There's nobody here," says Geoffrey, looking up and down

the street. "I can't see anything except icecream all over the path."

"That must be where your icecream dripped," says Bungle. "Max must have followed your icecream trail,

"But how are we going to do that?" asks George. "We don't know where the little girl lives, or even what her name is."

Geoffrey smiles. "I think I know a way of finding out," he says.

Zippy. I think he must be lost."

"I think so too," says Geoffrey. "I think we should try and find out where he lives, so that we can take him back. The little girl will be very unhappy that he's lost."

"What is it?" asks Zippy. "How are you going to find out?"

"Wait and see!" says Geoffrey.

He picks up the puppy and brings him inside.

"Now," says Geoffrey, "we'll find out where this puppy comes from by looking at his collar."

"At his collar?" says George. "How does that help?"

Geoffrey shows them the little dog's collar. There is a metal tag hanging on it. There is writing on the tag.

"I think that this will tell us where to take him," he says, smiling.

"Oh, yes!" says Zippy. "It says, 'Max, 32 Park Road'."

"That's not very far away," says Bungle. "We could take him back now. It wouldn't take very long, and then we can be back in time for tea."

"Goody, goody!" says Zippy greedily.

So off they go to 32 Park Road.

When they get there, Geoffrey knocks at the front door, and the little girl opens it.

"Hello," says Bungle. "We

found Max outside our door. We think he followed our icecream trail."

The little girl is very pleased to see that Max is safe and well. "He ran away from me when we were in the park," she says. "I didn't know where he had gone. Oh, thank you for bringing him back! Will you come in and have some tea?"

"Oh, yes please!" says Zippy. So they go inside the little girl's house, where her mummy gives them all sandwiches and cakes, and then as a special treat – icecream! Max sits on the floor beside the table, and has his own plate with icecream on it, so that he doesn't try to eat Zippy's! When they have finished eating, they help the little girl and her mummy to clear away the plates and bowls, and then they all go outside into the sunshine to play in the garden. And this time, they make sure that the gate is shut, so that Max can't get out and run away again.

"What a lovely day!" says George as they walk home.

"Yes, it was," says Bungle.

"Oh, yes!" says Zippy, licking his lips. "Two lots of icecream in one day! Yum, yum!"

Where Does Max Live?

To find out where Max lives, Geoffrey looks at the puppy's collar. He finds a name tag with the address "32 Park Road" written on it. They all decide to take Max back to his owner. It's not very far. Can you show them the best way to the little girl's house?

32
SCHOOL
PARK ROAD
ICE CREAM

Picture ABC

Look at the pictures and read the words.

a A alligator

b B Bungle

c C car

d D dog

e E egg

f F frog

g G George

h H house

i I igloo

j J jug

k K kangaroo

l L lake

m M mummy

n N numbers

o O owl

p P pencil

q Q queen

r R rose

s S snowman

t T tree

Make a picture ABC with your own words.

Easter Bonnets

"Do you know what day it is on Sunday?" asks Bungle.

"Is it your birthday?" asks George.

"No! But it's a special day. It's Easter Day," says Bungle.

"Why is it a special day?" asks Zippy.

"Well, on this day some people go to church to pray and give their thanks for a man named Jesus who, a long time ago, rose up after he had died," says Bungle.

"Easter is a time for many people to celebrate with a lot of good things," says Zippy.

"Yes!" says Bungle. "Eating chocolate Easter Eggs and hot cross buns, and wearing Easter bonnets."

"Easter is a time to celebrate," says George.

"To celebrate Jesus rising up from the dead and for the coming of springtime, and all the flowers."

"Let *us* celebrate," says George.

"We could have a party," says Bungle. "We could invite Geoffrey, and all our other friends. Maybe they'd like to wear hats too."

"Oh, what a good idea!" says George. "Shall we start making our hats now?"

"Let's make invitations for everyone first," says Bungle, and they set to work making invitations out of coloured card and writing everyone's name on them.

Then Geoffrey comes in. "Hello," he says. "What are you doing?"

"Well," says George, "we thought we'd have a party on Sunday, Geoffrey, because it's a special day, Easter Day. We're making invitations."

"That's a very good idea," says Geoffrey. "Are you going to make Easter bonnets?"

"What are bonnets?" asks Zippy.

"A bonnet is the same thing as a hat," says Bungle. "It's another word for it."

"Easter bonnets!" says George. "I think bonnet is a much better word than hat, don't you, Zippy?"

"Yes," says Zippy, "and I'm going to make sure that my bonnet is the best!"

"No, you're not," says George. "I am!"

"Why don't we make it an Easter bonnet party?" says Geoffrey. "Everyone has to make an Easter bonnet, and the nicest one wins a prize!"

"What's the prize going to be?" asks Zippy.

"Wait and see!" laughs Geoffrey.

All the next day, Bungle, Zippy and George get ready for their party. They find some old hats that nobody wants, and they make little flowers out of tissue paper and stick them on to the hats.

"I think my hat is nicer than yours," says Zippy to George.

"No, it isn't," says George. "What do you think, Bungle?"

"I think they're both very nice," says Bungle. "But we don't know what other people's bonnets are going to be like, do we?"

"No, we don't," says George. "So we don't know who's going to win the prize, do we? Isn't it exciting?"

When everyone comes to the party, they are all wearing lovely Easter bonnets. Some have flowers in, some have little chickens made of balls of wool,

and some have big ribbons tied into bows. George thinks they're all lovely.

"Who do you think will win the prize?" he asks.

"Well, I think they're all very good," says Zippy. "But I think mine is the best."

"Geoffrey will choose the winner," says Bungle. "Let's have some sandwiches and cakes, shall we, before he chooses?"

Everyone sits down at the table, and they eat everything up.

"I'm still hungry," says Zippy, looking to see if there are any crisps left.

"Well, we've eaten everything," says Bungle. "And you ate most!"

Geoffrey laughs. "Don't worry. I have the feeling that there will be something else to eat in a little while!"

"Oh, what, what?" asks Zippy, but Geoffrey won't tell him just yet.

"Now," says Bungle, "shall we have the Easter bonnet competition?"

"That's a good idea, Bungle," says George. "Then we'll know who's won the prize!"

"It'll be me!" says Zippy. "Ha ha! Me, me, me!"

"Come on, then," says Geoffrey. "Everyone must stand in a line, and I'll walk up and down. Then I'll tell you who's the winner!"

Everyone stands in a long line, and Geoffrey walks up and down and looks at everyone's Easter bonnet.

"Now," he says when he's

seen them all, "I've got a surprise for you. All the bonnets are so good that I've decided to give everyone a prize!"

"Oh, what a good idea!" says Bungle.

"What are the prizes?" asks Zippy. "Come on, Geoffrey, tell us, tell us!"

"These!" says Geoffrey, laughing. He opens a big bag he has brought with him, and takes out lots of chocolate eggs. He gives one to each of the people at the party.

"Oh, lovely!" says Zippy, who is very pleased. "I'm going to eat mine now!"

"You would!" laughs Bungle. "I think I'll eat a bit of mine, and save the rest for tomorrow."

"And me!" says George. "Thank you, Geoffrey!"

"Yes, thank you, Geoffrey," says everyone. "It *has* been a lovely party!"

Easter Cards

How many Easter cards has Geoffrey got? His favourite card is the one sent from Bungle, George and Zippy. They made it themselves. This is what they did:-

What they needed

two yellow cotton wool balls
non-toxic glue
a piece of thin card
paper to draw on
round-ended scissors
a pencil

What they did

1 Fold the card in half.
2 Stick a blob of cotton wool onto the front of the card to make the chick's body.
3 Stick another blob of cotton wool in position as the chick's head.
4 Draw the chick's round eyes on paper and colour them in. Cut them out and stick them down on the head where you think they should go.

5 Draw a beak (a triangle-shape) on paper and colour it in. Cut out the beak and stick it down in position.
6 Draw the chick's feet and legs on the card below its body.
7 Draw an egg-shape on paper and cut it out.
8 Cut across the middle of the egg in zig-zags to make it look as though it's broken.
9 Stick the egg-shapes onto the card.

Reflections

Bungle, George and Zippy are clearing away the dishes after lunch. Bungle is telling everyone what to do, "I will wash, Zippy can do the drying, and George, you can put everything away," he says.

They have almost finished. Zippy is drying a tablespoon when he says with surprise, "Oh, look! I can see myself in this spoon, but I look funny. I'm upside-down."

"If you turn the spoon over, you will be the right way up," says Bungle.

"Oh yes, but I look even funnier this way," says Zippy.

"Let me see," says George and he leans over Zippy's shoulder.

Bungle explains to them both that what they are looking at is called a reflection. It is a reflection of themselves.

Look for *your* reflection.

Look into a spoon

Look into a window

Look into a puddle

Look into a mirror

Reflections are clearer in things that are smooth and shiny. Is this true?

Let's Go Shopping

Bungle, George and Zippy are doing their weekly shopping.

"We need some bread, Bungle," says Zippy, reading from the top of the shopping list. "But where do we go to get bread?"

"We get bread from the baker's," says George.

"Or we could get bread from the supermarket," says Bungle.

"We need toothpaste too," says Zippy. "Where do we go to get toothpaste?"

Can you help our friends to find what they need on their shopping list? Read down the list, and tell them where they can buy each thing.

GREENGROCER
CHEMIST
BAKER
BUTCHER
SUPERMARKET

A Tat the Cat story . . .

by Audrey and Bill Titcombe

CUDDLES

When Tat woke up he had a headache and he felt a bit sick, so his first thought was to go to Alexander. But Alexander was not in the barn.

Then he looked for Oscar, but Oscar was not there either!

"Oh dear," he said to himself, "I do feel lonely. I think I will go back to bed." And he did.

Later on the three posh ducks came in to the barn for their lunch.

Prunella looked across at Tat. "What's wrong with you?" she called.

"I'm not very well," said Tat.

"Oh, you are just feeling sorry for yourself," said Prunella. "Why don't you get up and go and see Poppet? She will make a fuss of you and cheer you up."

Tat made his way across the farmyard, then he went through the little door and into the farmhouse.

Poppet was in her basket, and lying beside her was a tiny puppy. Poppet smiled at Tat. "Hello," she said, "this is Chas, the latest addition to the household."

Tat looked at the little dog. "Why is he crying?" he asked.

"Because he misses his mother," replied Poppet.

"I am giving him a kiss and a cuddle," said Poppet. "He will soon feel better."

Tat thought that he would like a cuddle, too, but Poppet was too busy with Chas to take any notice of him.

As Tat left the farmhouse it started to rain, so he went and sheltered with Esmerelda, who was lying down with her babies.

''Hello, Tat dear,'' she said. ''We are just having a cuddle after lunch. After a cuddle my babies soon go to sleep, and then I can have a rest.''

Tat waited until the rain had stopped, said, "Goodbye," to Esmerelda, then made his way back to the barn.

Oscar was pleased to see Tat, but he could tell that the little cat was not very happy. "Would you like to tell me what is wrong?" he asked kindly.

Tat sat down and explained about everyone else being cuddled and not him.

The three posh ducks started to giggle.

Oscar glared at them. "Everyone needs a cuddle from time to time," he said. "So be quiet!"

Oscar went over to Tat and put his paw around him, and in no time Tat felt much better, and very happy indeed.

Fireworks

Bungle, Zippy and George are very excited today, because it's the fifth of November – and that means it's Bonfire Night!

"When will it get dark?" asks Zippy, looking out of the window.

"Soon," says Bungle. "You see, Zippy, it's almost winter, and in winter it gets dark much earlier than it does in summer. It will be dark about tea-time."

"Will it be tea-time soon?" asks Zippy. "I'm hungry!"

"You're always hungry," laughs Bungle. "Yes, it will soon be tea-time, and then we can go to the bonfire."

"Oh, yes," says George. "Wasn't it a good idea, Bungle, to have a bonfire for the whole street?"

"Yes, it was," says Bungle. "It means that everyone gets to see lots and lots of lovely fireworks, and it stops people playing with them and getting hurt."

"Fireworks can be dangerous, so it's best for everyone to stand far away from them," says Zippy.

"Mr Brown and Mrs Roberts will light them, so that everyone can see, and be safe," says Bungle.

"That's a good idea," says Zippy. "Is it tea-time yet?"

It is, so they all sit down and have their tea.

When they've finished, Zippy looks out of the window. "Oh, look, George, it's dark!" he says.

"Oh yes!" says George. "Is it time to go to the bonfire, Bungle?"

"Yes, it is," says Bungle. "We must wrap up well, because it's cold outside."

So they put on their hats and scarves and gloves and go along to the park where the bonfire is. There are many

people already there, waiting for the bonfire to be lit, and the fireworks to begin.

Nearby there is a man selling hot dogs. Zippy's eyes light up.

"Oh, Zippy," says George. "You've only just had your tea!"

"You can't be hungry again," says Bungle, laughing. "Wait until we've seen the fireworks, and then maybe we'll have a hot dog each."

"Oh look," says George. "There's Mrs Smith from next door. Hello, Mrs Smith. Have you come to see the fireworks?"

"Hello, you three," says Mrs Smith. "Yes, I wouldn't miss it for anything."

"Have you brought your dog, Henry?" asks Zippy. "He'd like to see the fireworks too, wouldn't he?"

"I don't think he would," says Mrs Smith. "I've left him at home tonight. You see, pets don't like bright lights and loud noises. Henry would be frightened."

"Oh, poor Henry," says George. "It was a good idea, then, to leave him at home."

"Look," says Zippy. "Mr Brown is lighting the bonfire!"

"Yes, it is," says George, whose eyes are as big as saucers. "Bungle, what's that on top of the bonfire? It looks like a person. It isn't, is it?"

"No, no," laughs Bungle. "That's the guy."

"The what?" asks Zippy.

"The guy," says Bungle. "It's made of old clothes stuffed full of paper and rubbish. You always put a guy on the bonfire on Bonfire Night."

"Why?" asks George.

The bonfire is very big. Everyone has brought along bits of paper and old wood, and now the bonfire is lit. It soon starts to burn.

"There's Mr Roberts," says Bungle. "Look, he's going to start lighting the fireworks!"

Mr Roberts lights a firework called Silver Rain, then moves away from it. It's very big. There are popping noises, and then the firework throws out lots and lots of silver lights that fall to the ground.

"Pop! Pop!" shouts Zippy. "Isn't that lovely, George?"

"Well," says Mrs Smith. "A long time ago there were some people who didn't like what the king was doing and they wanted to get rid of him by putting gunpowder into the cellars under the Houses of Parliament to blow it up. One of the men who wanted to kill the king was named Guy Fawkes."

"Oh, I've heard of him," says George. "Is that why we put a guy on the bonfire? Is it named after Guy Fawkes?"

"That's right," says Mrs Smith. "We remember the Gunpowder Plot on Bonfire Night."

"And fireworks can sound like things being blown up," says Zippy.

"We don't use gunpowder today, but something that makes a bang," says Mrs Smith. "Look, Mr Roberts is going to light a rocket. It will go up into the air, then it goes bang, and all the stars come out."

Mr Roberts lights the end of the rocket. After a moment,

there's a very loud whizzing noise, and the rocket shoots up into the sky!

"Ooooh!" shouts everyone.

"Whizz, whizz!" says Zippy, jumping up and down.

"Bang!" goes the rocket in the sky, and a lot of red and green and blue and gold stars shoot out of it.

"Aaaaah!" shouts everyone.

"Isn't it lovely?" says George. "Are there any more?"

"Lots and lots!" says Bungle. "Look, there are Roman candles, and whizz-bangs, and crackers, and all sorts of others!"

"Goody goody!" says Zippy.

George, Zippy and Bungle watch the fireworks. There are lots of bright lights, red, gold, silver, blue, green and purple, and whizzing, popping, whirring, fizzing noises. All the people are shouting, "Ooooh!" and, "Aaaah!" and shouting and laughing. Everyone is having fun.

"I like Bonfire Night!" says George.

"So do I," says Zippy. "It's so exciting!"

"I like it too," says Bungle. "What a pity we don't have Bonfire Night every day!"

At last the firework display is over, and people start to go home.

"I'm still hungry," says Zippy, looking at the man selling hot dogs.

"I am too," says George, smiling.

"All right," laughs Bungle. "We'll have a hot dog each!"

And so they do. What a lovely Bonfire Night!

Bungle's Bonfire Picture

Bungle is showing George and Zippy how to make a bonfire picture. You can make one too.

What you need

a piece of card
some brightly-coloured wax crayons
a black wax crayon
an object with a blunt, but pointed edge, to be used as a scraper
a sheet of newspaper
a flat table on which to work

What you do

1 Lay the newspaper flat on the table.

2 Put everything you need on top of the newspaper.

3 With a bright crayon draw some lines across the card from edge to edge. Your lines don't need to be straight, but you must leave a space between them.

4 Colour in the spaces between the lines with brightly-coloured wax crayons

5 Now take the black crayon, and pressing down fairly hard, go over the bright colours. A thick layer of black should completely cover the bright colours.

6 By carefully scraping away the black wax from the bright colours underneath, scrape out a bonfire, fireworks and people.

7 Collect the bits of wax in the newspaper and throw this away.

Make a Zippy Puppet

Would you like to make a puppet that looks just like Zippy? Read the instructions carefully and look at the drawings. It may seem difficult, but if you ask a grown-up to help, it can be quite easy.

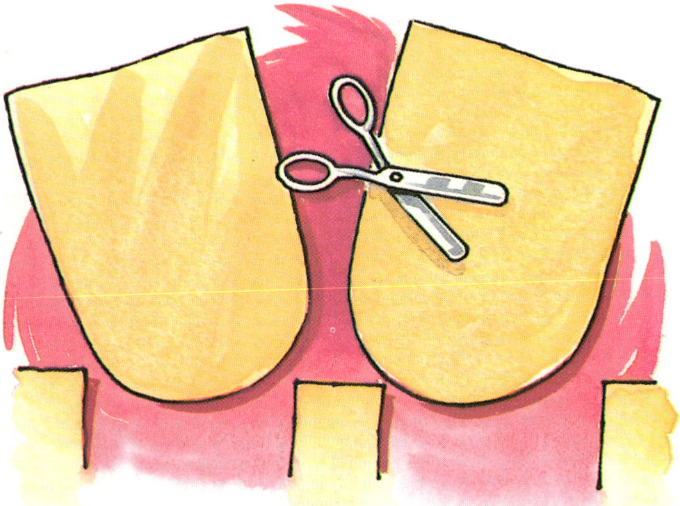

What you need

paper to use as a pattern
yellow felt for the head and face
black felt for the mouth
white felt for the corner of the mouth
pink felt for the tongue
white, blue, and black felt for the eyes
round-ended scissors
a needle and sewing thread
a pencil
a flat surface on which to work
a grown-up to help with the cutting and sewing

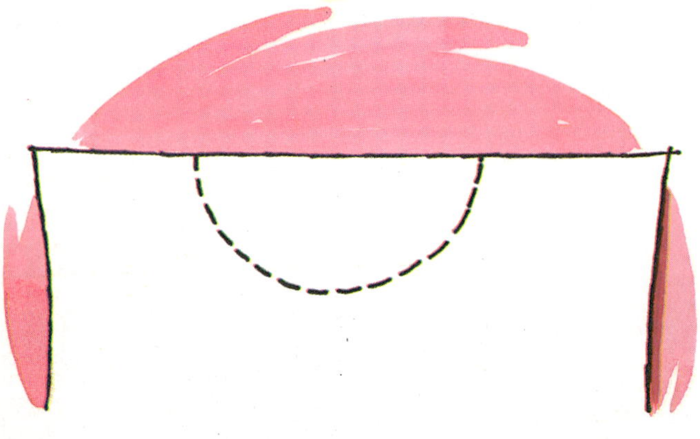

What you do

1
Place you hand flat on the paper, and with a pencil draw a line around your hand to make a paper pattern. Make the pattern slightly larger than the size of your hand.

2
Place the pattern on the yellow felt and cut out two pieces for the head and face.

3
Make another paper pattern for the mouth using the head pattern, but this time only cut round the curved part.

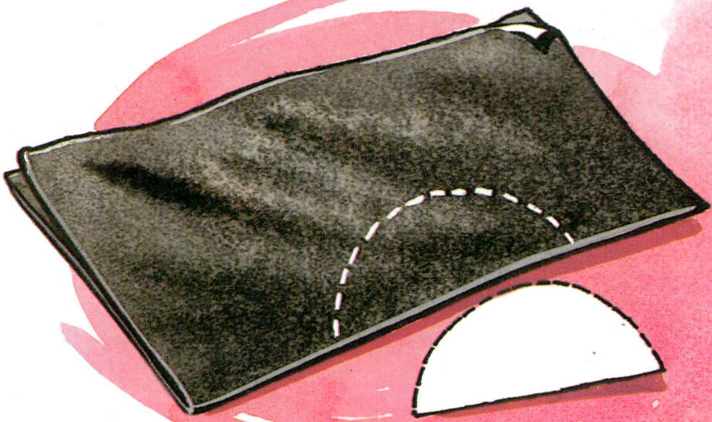

4
Fold the black felt. Place the straight edge of the mouth pattern on the fold, and draw round the curved edge.
5
Keeping the felt folded, cut round the curved edge, and mark the fold lightly before opening it out.
6
Cut out a tongue-shape from the pink felt and sew the straight edge along the middle of the mouth.
7
Now for the eyes – cut out two white ovals, two smaller blue ovals, and two small black ovals.
8
Position the eyes on the face piece and sew.
9
Pin half of the mouth to the face piece and sew round the curve to the half-way mark.
10
Pin the other half of the mouth to the plain head piece and sew round the curve.
11
Join up the side seams.
12
Cut out a ring of white felt and sew this to the right side of Zippy's mouth.

The Grasshopper and the Elephant

Way down south where bananas grow,
A grasshopper stepped on an elephant's toe.
The elephant said, with tears in his eyes,
"Pick on somebody your own size!"

What did the elephant mean when he said this?

At the Burger Bar

Bungle, Zippy and George are shopping in town, and now it's lunchtime. They're all hungry – especially Zippy!

"Shall we go home and have something to eat?" asks George.

"Well, we could," says Bungle, "except that I told Geoffrey we'd meet him a bit later on, and if we go home we'll be late."

"I'm hungry," says Zippy. "Aren't we going to eat anything?"

Bungle laughs. "Ha ha! Of course we are," he says. "I thought we could eat something here in town."

"But how can we do that?" asks George. "We didn't bring any sandwiches, Bungle."

"No," says Bungle, laughing. "I didn't mean

sandwiches. Why don't we go to the Burger Bar?"

"What's that?" asks Zippy. "What's a Burger Bar, Bungle?"

"It's a place where you can buy fast food—hamburgers, and chips, and salads, and all sorts of things to eat," says Bungle. "You can take them away with you, and eat them in a park or somewhere like that, or you can sit down inside the Burger Bar and eat them there."

"Oh, what a good idea!" says Zippy. "Let's go to the Burger Bar!"

And so they go to the Burger Bar. It is a place that looks a bit like a shop, but it has tables and chairs, where everyone sits down and has their lunch. There are a lot of people there, and there is a girl behind the counter wearing a red dress and a little red hat with 'BB' on the front.

"Hello," she says. "What would you like to eat?"

"What have you got?" asks greedy Zippy.

The girl laughs. "We've got hamburgers, some with cheese on top, and salads, and milk shakes, and lemonade . . ."

Zippy's eyes grow bigger and bigger as she tells them what there is to eat.

"I'd like a hamburger with cheese on it, please," says George. "And can I have a

strawberry milk shake, please, Bungle?"

"Yes, you can, George," says Bungle. "I'd like a plain hamburger, please, with salad. What about you, Zippy?"

"Can I have a hamburger with cheese on it, and some chips?" asks Zippy. "And a chocolate milk shake, too, please."

"You must be very hungry," laughs the girl behind the counter. Her name is Linda.

"Yes, I am," says Zippy. "I'm

so hungry that I could eat all that, *and* George's hamburger, *and* Bungle's too."

"Well, you eat your own hamburger first," says Bungle, laughing, "and then we'll see if you're still hungry, Zippy."

He gives Linda some money for the food, and she gives him some change.

"Now," says Bungle to George and Zippy, "watch this, and you'll see what I mean about fast food."

Linda goes to a warm shelf just behind the counter. On it there are little plastic boxes. Some have red writing on them and some have blue writing on them. She takes two boxes with red writing on them, and one with blue writing on it, and puts them on a tray. Then she goes to another part of the shelf, and takes a little plastic carton from it. She puts that on the tray too. Finally, she reaches underneath the counter, and brings out two

tall plastic beakers with lids on, and straws sticking out of the top.

She brings the tray back to the counter and gives it to Bungle.

"But where's our food?" says Zippy.

Bungle and Linda laugh. "It's in all these little boxes," says Linda. "You see, in the Burger Bar, we cook everything before you come in, and then put it on those hot shelves to keep warm until you come in and buy it."

"I now know what you mean about fast food," says George. If we are in a real hurry, we don't have to wait for it."

"That's right," says Bungle. "Thank you, Linda. Now, Zippy and George, shall we go and eat our burgers?"

"That's a good idea," says Zippy.

They go to a table and sit down, and Bungle gives

George and Zippy the boxes with red writing on them. He takes the one with blue writing on it. Inside there is a plain hamburger and a salad. George and Zippy open their boxes and find their hamburgers with cheese. Then Bungle gives Zippy the little carton. Inside there are lots of hot chips.

"Where's my milkshake?" asks Zippy.

"Here you are," says Bungle, and he gives each of them one of the plastic beakers. Zippy's chocolate milkshake has brown writing on the outside, and George's strawberry milkshake has pink writing on the outside.

"They put different coloured writing on so that you can tell what's inside," says Bungle.

"Oh, I see," says George. "Chocolate is brown, so that's why the writing is brown, too."

"And strawberries are pinky red, so the writing is pink!" says Zippy. "That's clever!"

Then they all eat their lunch.

"This is lovely," says George, munching his hamburger.